REALM OF THE PANTHER

A Story of South Florida's Forests

by Emily Costello

Illustrated by Wes Siegrist

Soundprints
Where Children Discover...

For my brothers: Michael, John, and Patrick—E.C.

Dedicated to my wife, Rachelle—for your input, assistance,
and ever joyful companionship—W.S.

Book copyright © 2000 Soundprints, a division of Trudy Corporation,
353 Main Avenue, Norwalk, CT 06851.

Soundprints is a division of Trudy Corporation, Norwalk, Connecticut.

Book layout: Scott Findlay
Editor: Judy Gitenstein
Art Director: Diane Hinze Kanzler

First edition 2000
10 9 8 7 6 5 4 3 2 1
Printed in Hong Kong

Acknowledgments:
  Our thanks to David Maehr of the University of Kentucky's Department of Forestry
for his curatorial review.

Library of Congress Cataloging - in - Publication Data

Costello, Emily
    Realm of the panther: a story of South Florida's forests / by Emily Costello;
illustrated by Wes Seigrist. — 1st ed.
        p.   cm.
    Summary: In Florida's Big Cypress National Preserve, two hungry panther kittens
go in search of food and succeed in their first hunt without their mother.
    ISBN 1-56899-847-3 (hardcover) — ISBN 1-56899-848-1 (pbk.)
    1. Florida panther—Juvenile fiction. [1. Florida panther—fiction.
    2. Pumas—Fiction. 3. Animals—Infancy—Fiction.] I. Seigrist, Wes, ill. II. Title.

PZ10.3.C8198 Re 2000
[Fic] — dc21
                                                                                            99-043775
                                                                                                 CIP
                                                                                                  AC

REALM OF THE PANTHER

A Story of South Florida's Forests

by Emily Costello

Illustrated by Wes Siegrist

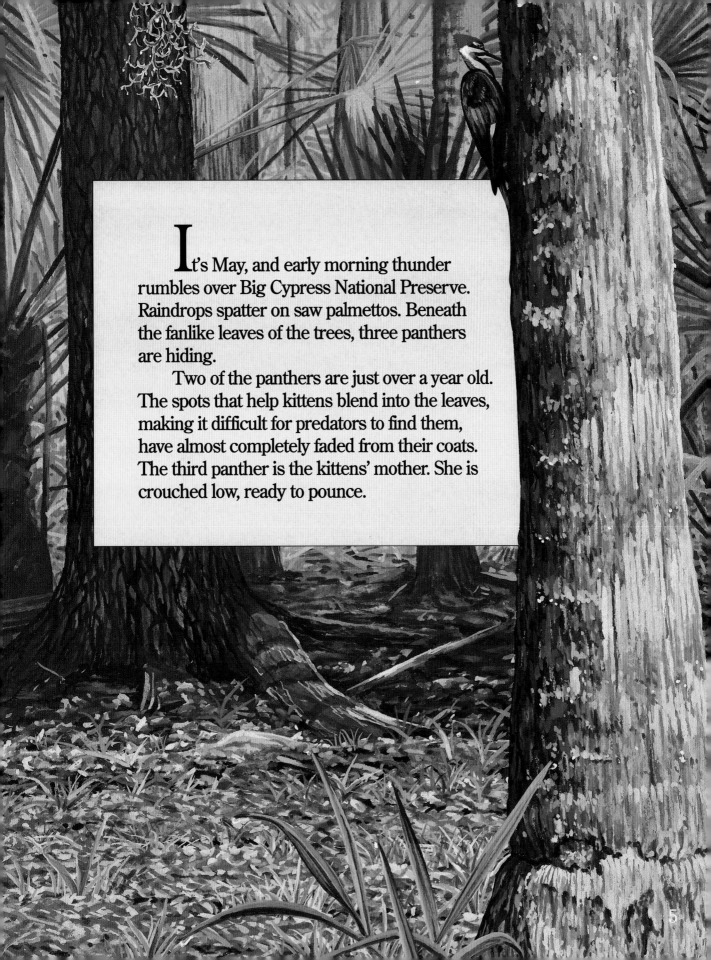

It's May, and early morning thunder rumbles over Big Cypress National Preserve. Raindrops spatter on saw palmettos. Beneath the fanlike leaves of the trees, three panthers are hiding.

Two of the panthers are just over a year old. The spots that help kittens blend into the leaves, making it difficult for predators to find them, have almost completely faded from their coats. The third panther is the kittens' mother. She is crouched low, ready to pounce.

A few yards away, a wild hog grunts softly as he digs in the moist soil for roots to eat. The male kitten's muscles itch to move. Both kittens are almost old enough to hunt. But for now, the mother lets them share the food she catches. So, as clouds of mosquitoes drone in the humid air, the kittens do nothing but wait and watch.

The male sees a sudden blur of tan-gray fur. His mother has attacked the hog! Growling, the hog turns and fights back. But the mother bites the hog's neck, breaking its spine.

As soon as the hog is dead, the young panthers come out of hiding. All three panthers feed until their bellies stick out. Then, feeling sleepy, they paw a mound of sticks, dirt, and leaves over the hog.

The sun is high. The mother and kittens
pant in the simmering heat. They slowly pad
toward a hardwood hammock, a small piece of
land that rises above the shallow water flooding
the surrounding wet prairie.

Crouching low, the panthers crawl beneath
a thick-growing tangle of oak trees and cabbage
palm. Here, the animals are protected from the
heat and glare of the sun.

The panther family settles in for a nap. Even
as the young panther dozes, his sensitive ears pick
up sounds: A lizard scuttling through strap fern,
the buzzing of mosquitos, the musical sound of
trilling Carolina wrens.

The sun is setting when the panther and his sister wake and stretch. He licks a paw, and uses it to smooth the fur on his face. She brushes twigs, dirt, and leaves off her belly with her rough tongue.

The kittens' mother is gone. She often disappears for a day or two to hunt alone.

13

The young panthers return to the hog.
A raccoon is gnawing at their dinner! The young
female lunges forward with a growl. Frightened,
the raccoon scurries away.

When the male's stomach is full again,
he slowly creeps up on his sister...and pounces!
The kittens wrestle and growl. They are doing
more than playing—they're practicing their
hunting skills.

15

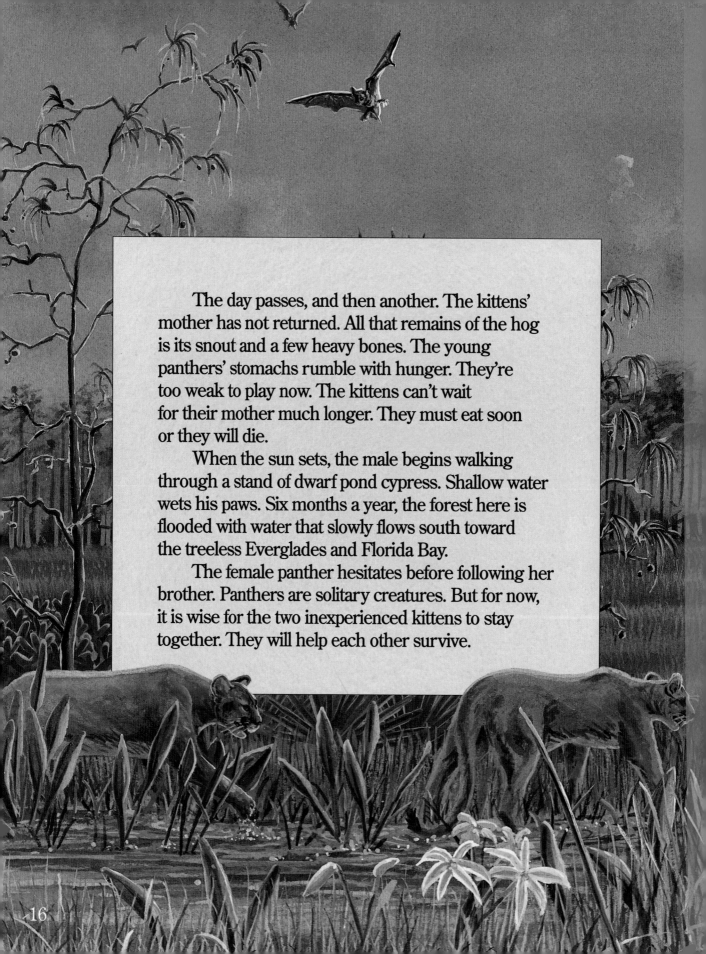

The day passes, and then another. The kittens' mother has not returned. All that remains of the hog is its snout and a few heavy bones. The young panthers' stomachs rumble with hunger. They're too weak to play now. The kittens can't wait for their mother much longer. They must eat soon or they will die.

When the sun sets, the male begins walking through a stand of dwarf pond cypress. Shallow water wets his paws. Six months a year, the forest here is flooded with water that slowly flows south toward the treeless Everglades and Florida Bay.

The female panther hesitates before following her brother. Panthers are solitary creatures. But for now, it is wise for the two inexperienced kittens to stay together. They will help each other survive.

The young panthers walk ten miles without stopping. At the edge of a slash pine stand, the panthers sense movement. They stop and sink to a crouch.

A white-tailed deer is feeding on buttonbush. The female panther takes a step closer. She stops, waits, watches. She takes another step. The wind shifts, carrying the panther's scent to the doe. Startled, the doe raises her head. She bounds away, her white tail flashing.

A few miles farther on, the kittens catch the scent of adult male panther. The smell is coming from a pile of scraped-together leaves. This pile marks the beginning of the adult male's home territory. The young panthers turn away. They don't want a fight—especially when they are weak with hunger.

Too late! An adult panther charges out of the palmettos and jumps onto the male kitten. The young panther crashes over onto his side.

21

Rushing forward, the female kitten bats the older panther with her paw. Then she turns and runs. The male kitten scrambles to his feet and follows her.

The kittens stop running as soon as they sense the older panther isn't chasing them. The young male's ear is bleeding. He licks his paw and touches the wound with it. He lies down on his belly and the female kitten licks at the wound until the blood stops. The male's hunger is greater than his pain, though. Soon the panthers are on the move again, hunting for food.

The male hears a thrashing sound among drying red maple leaves. He crouches, body tense and ready. A nine-banded armadillo is feeding near a thicket of saw palmetto. She is using her strong, curved claws to dig termites out of a half-rotten log.

The male panther steps forward. The armadillo licks up bugs with her long tongue.

The panther lunges. The armadillo sees him and runs for her burrow. She's too slow! The panther stretches out one massive paw and pulls her closer. The armadillo draws in her feet. Bony plates covering her back and tail now surround her. The panther paws at her until he flips her over. He sinks his teeth right through the bony shell—just as he watched his mother do many times.

The female creeps forward eagerly. The kittens' first hunt is a success. Later, when the sun is hot, they will sleep without hunger.

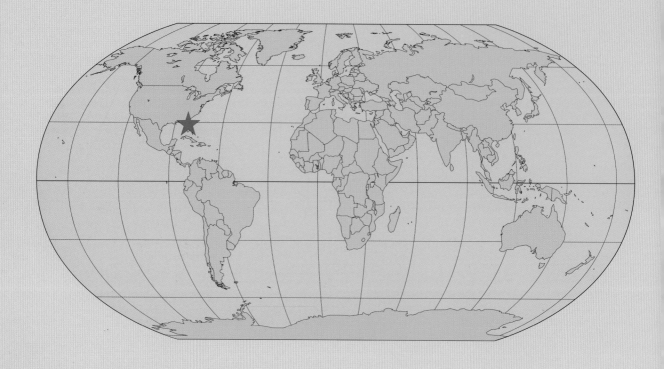

South Florida, United States

South Florida boasts several unique ecosystems. Big Cypress National Preserve is dominated by a seasonally flooded cypress forest. Here you can see orchids and live oak trees with hanging moss. South Florida is home to panthers, bobcats, black bears, and, in recent years, the coyote.

About Southern Florida

The story in this book takes place in the Big Cypress National Preserve, a land of slash pine, hardwood hammocks, wet prairies, dry prairies, marshes, and mangrove forests in southern Florida. The Preserve is home to the Florida panther, one of twenty-six subspecies of panthers that live in North and South America. The range of the Florida panther covers the forested areas of Collier, Hendry, Lee, Monroe, Dade, and Broward Counties.

Panthers have more names than any other animal in the world. Some of the names include cougar, mountain lion, puma, and catamount.

All of Florida's panthers are protected under the Endangered Species Act, but some scientists are uncertain if this population can remain healthy for long.

Scientists estimate that as few as seventy or eighty Florida panthers remain. Most live in the Big Cypress Preserve and on private land surrounding the Preserve. About five panthers live south of Big Cypress in Everglades National Park. This smaller population has difficulty surviving because there is so little forest cover in the Everglades and food is hard to find. Both populations are cut off from the rest of Florida and the United States by the Caloosahatchee River which stretches from Fort Myers to Lake Okeechobee.

More farms and homes are being built in south Florida every day. In fact, it seems likely that the panthers' habitat will be reduced further in the future. Land in southern Florida is in great demand. Each week more than 5,000 people move to Florida, making it one of the nation's fastest growing states. New residents mean less room for the Florida panther.

Glossary

▲ Black-and-white warbler

▲ Lantana

▲ Saw palmetto

▲ Carolina wren

▲ Little green heron

▲ White-tailed deer

▲ Giant swallowtail butterfly

▲ Nine-banded armadillo

▲ Wild hog

▲ Great blue heron

▲ Red-shouldered hawk

▲ Wood stork

▲ String lily

▲ *Anhinga*

▲ *Common yellow throat*

▲ *Raccoon*

▲ *Banana spider*

▲ *Florida panther*

▲ *Spanish moss*

▲ *Barred owl*

▲ *Green anole*

▲ *Swallow-tailed kite*

▲ *Bromeliad*

▲ *Pileated woodpecker*

▲ *White ibis*

▲ *Pond cypress*